W9-BHV-094

SEA BEAR

A Journey for Survival

Lindsay Moore

Greenwillow Books
An Imprint of HarperCollins Publishers

This book would not have been possible without the work of intrepid scientists who traveled to remote study sites in Alaska, Canada, Greenland, Norway, and Russia to collect information about polar bears in the wild. With nearly fifty years' worth of peer-reviewed research published in books and scientific journals, we have a wealth of information available about polar bears. I'd like to thank Polar Bears International, for providing educational material about polar bears to the public in a clear and beautiful way. I would also like to thank Dr. Dale Smith, the planetarium director at Bowling Green State University, whose knowledge of polar astronomy informed my illustrations and opened my eyes to the wonders of the night sky.

Sea Bear: A Journey for Survival

Copyright © 2019 by Lindsay Moore. All rights reserved. Manufactured in Italy. For information address HarperCollins Children's Books, a division of HarperCollins Publishers, 195 Broadway, New York, NY 10007.
www.harpercollinschildrens.com

The full-color art was rendered in graphite, watercolor, drawing inks, conte crayon, and color pencils.
The text type is 18-point Brandon Text Bold.

Library of Congress Cataloging-in-Publication Data

Names: Moore, Lindsay, author, illustrator.
Title: Sea bear / written and illustrated by Lindsay Moore.
Description: First edition. | New York, NY :
Greenwillow Books, an Imprint of
HarperCollinsPublishers, [2019] |
Summary: A polar bear waits patiently for spring when the ice breaks up, but after months of hunting, paddling, and resting on ice floes, summer ends and the bear must swim very far to find land.
Includes facts about polar bears and the effect of climate change on their environment.
Identifiers: LCCN 2018004241 | ISBN 9780062791283 (hardcover) |
Subjects: LCSH: Polar bear—Juvenile fiction. | CYAC: Polar bear—Fiction. |
Bears—Fiction. | Climatic changes—Fiction. | Arctic regions—Fiction.
Classification: LCC PZ10.3.M7057 Se 2019 | DDC [E]—dc23 LC record available at https://lccn.loc.gov/2018004241

ISBN 978-0-06-279129-0 (paperback)

22 23 24 25 26 RTLO 10 9 8 7 6 5 4 3 2 1

First Greenwillow paperback, 2022

GREENWILLOW BOOKS

For my family.
With love,
L. M.

Polar bears are patient beasts,
as patient as glaciers.
We know how to hope and how to wait.
I learned to be patient long ago
from my polar bear mother—

to be patient when hunting,
to be patient with weather,
to be patient in darkness.

In spring the sun rises
and the ice breaks open.
I stalk seals out on the floes,

walking,   leaping,

slipping in and out
of deep water,

adding seal
after seal
to my stomach,
and resting.

A polar bear knows
how to take a good nap.

As summer ends, the ice is thin
and floes are far apart.
The young seals have grown fast.
They are wiser
and harder to catch.

They spread out with what's left of the ice.
I want to follow them, but I can't.

There is not enough ice left to hunt on.
Every day there is less ice to stand on.

A soft breeze from the south brings the smell of a beach.
It is faint, beyond sight, but I think I can reach it.

I am a sea bear. I am made to paddle—
under wandering Arctic terns,
    past lonely icebergs bobbing at the surface,
    and above the deep, dark shadow
    of a slow Arctic shark.

I swim with a school of star-skinned narwhals,

and paddle past a weary raft of wary walruses,

and glide over a whale
whose ancient songs
bubble up from darkness
in creaks and groans.

On the second night, the sky begins to change.
The waves grow in height
and the wind grows in wildness.

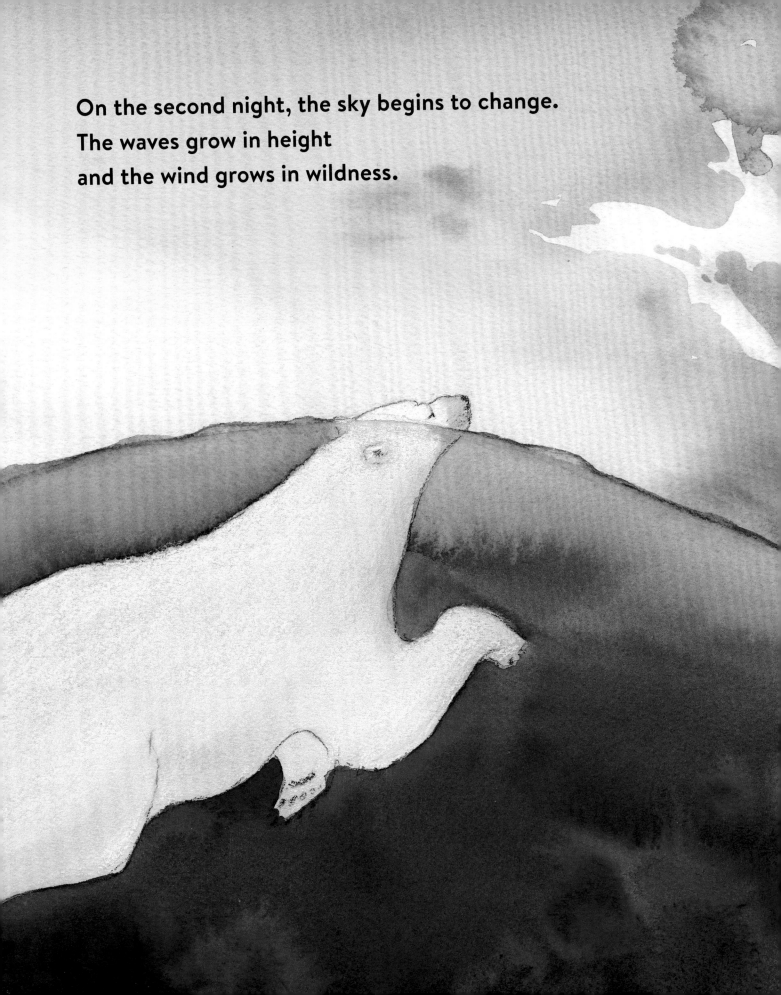

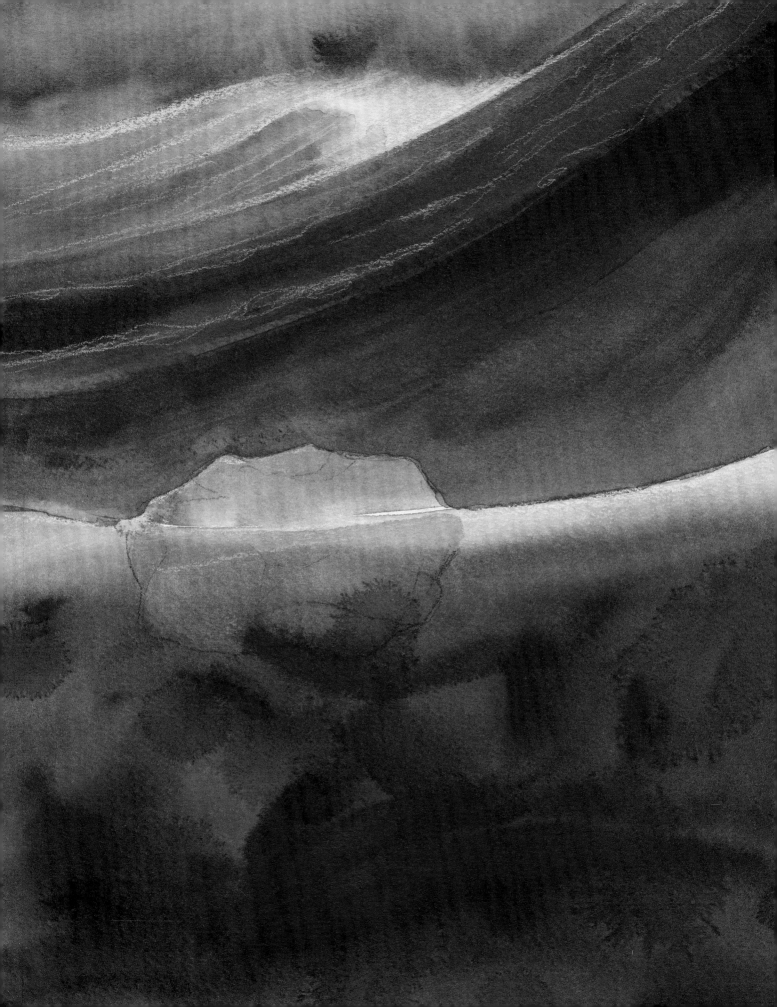

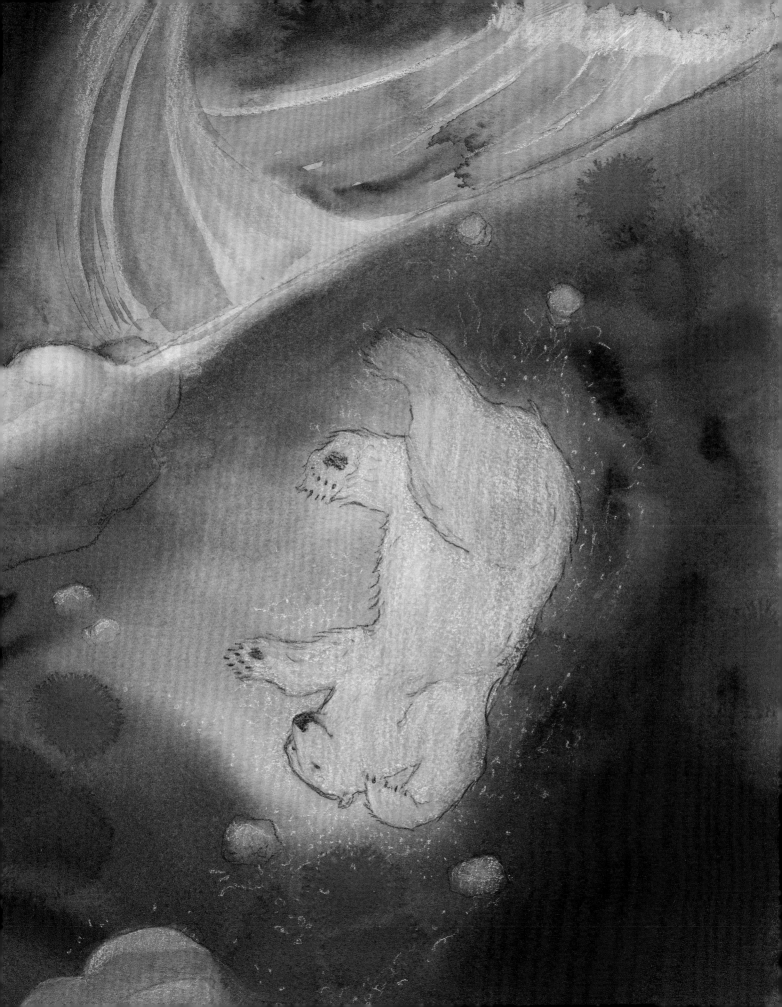

Tossed by a tempest
and nearly lost at sea,
I am tired
and wonder if I will ever reach land.

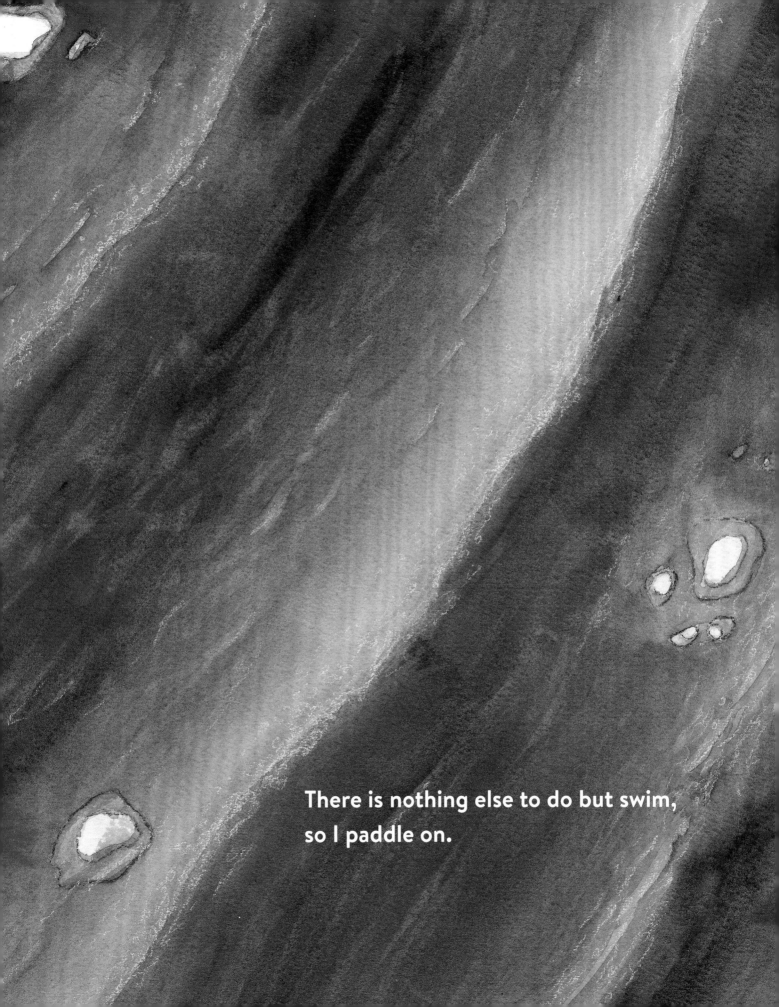

There is nothing else to do but swim,
so I paddle on.

On the third day,
the sea floor rises up beneath me.
Waves carry with them
the strong smell of soil.

Polar bears are not land bears.
We wait on land.
We hope on land.

But summer will end.

The sea will freeze again.

I will teach the sea's rhythm to my cubs
and whisper to them in the dark.
Polar bears are patient beasts,
as patient as glaciers.

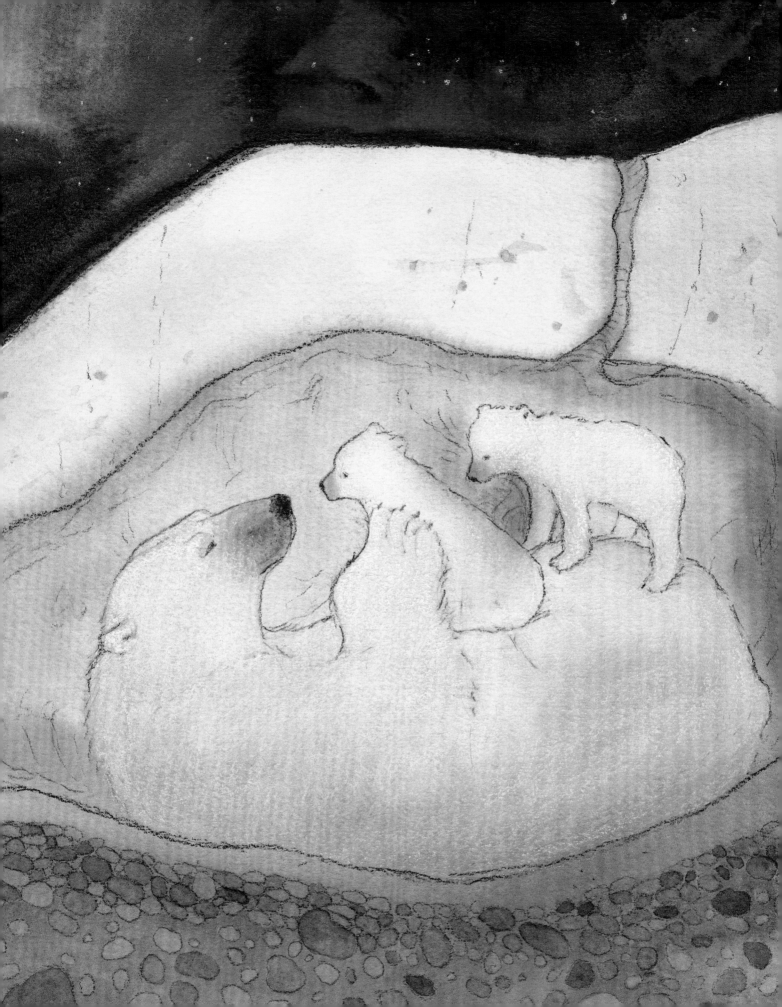

We know how to hope

and how to wait.

Sea Ice and Polar Bears

Sea ice is an important habitat for many Arctic animals. It forms on the sea surface when temperatures drop to 28.8 degrees Fahrenheit or below. Stronger and more flexible than freshwater ice, it is home to an estimated 26,000 polar bears who rely on its structure to walk, sleep, ride, and stalk seals over the deep sea.

Polar bears are well suited for life on sea ice. With wide, textured paws to provide traction and two layers of fur and a thick layer of body fat to keep warm, they can live and move comfortably in the winter when winds howl and the temperature can drop to as low as -50 degrees Fahrenheit. Sea ice moves with currents; it cracks open; it collides and it grows and melts with weather patterns and changing seasons. In summer, as the ice melts, the same paws that walked along the ice now make excellent paddles. Bears slip into water channels between ice to surprise sleeping seals, and can also swim across open water to find better places to hunt.

At the end of the summer, when the melting ice is no longer useful for hunting, many polar bears swim to shore. There they wait—living mostly off their body fat—until the temperature drops, the sea freezes again, and they can return to hunting seals. The bears that wait onshore the longest are pregnant bears. In the fall, they move farther inland and dig out dens in snowdrifts before their cubs are born in December. The family finally leaves for the ice in early spring.

Polar bears are good at living in a challenging environment, but things are getting harder. Air pollution is causing global climate change; our planet's overall temperature is rising. Warmer temperatures mean less and less sea ice in the Arctic. Scientists who study polar bears are noticing changes, too. With less ice there is more competition among the bears for food. With less ice, scientists are recording bears making longer swims over greater distances at the end of the summer. And once on land, polar bears are forced to fast longer while they wait for cold weather to return.

Polar bears have a remarkable life story. They are bears that make their home on top of the ocean. Their future, though, is tied to the future of sea ice. I wanted to give polar bears a voice, to tell what life is like for a bear in a changing Arctic landscape, and to inspire all of us to make changes in our own lives to slow climate change and help care for our earth.

Other Animals Above and Below the Ice

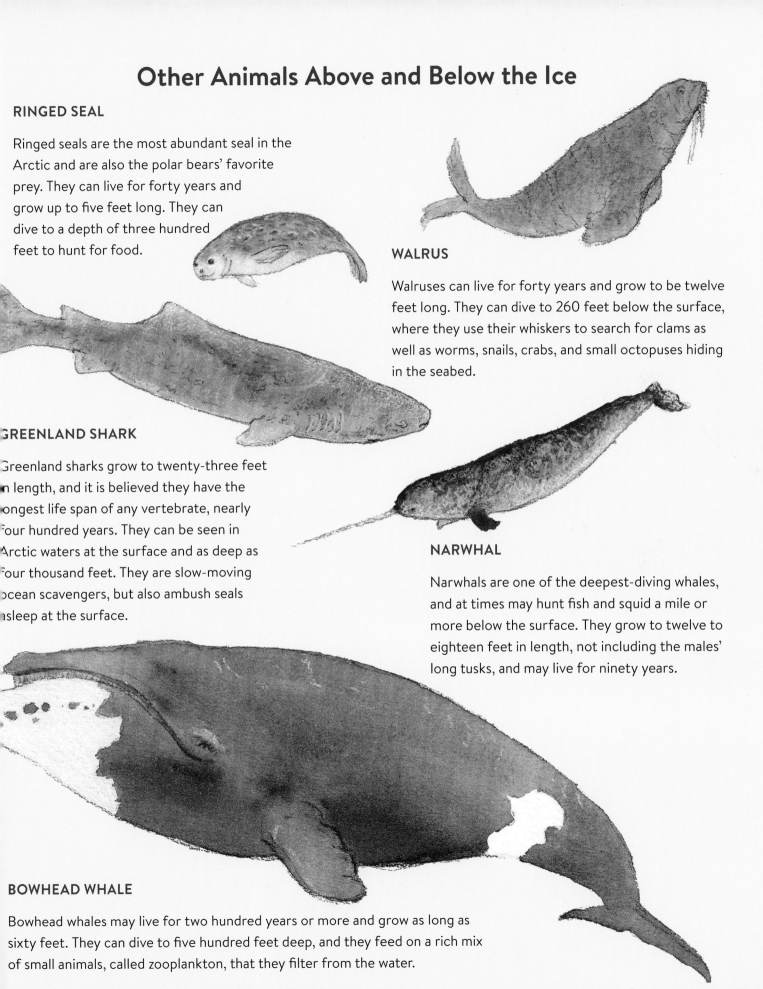

RINGED SEAL

Ringed seals are the most abundant seal in the Arctic and are also the polar bears' favorite prey. They can live for forty years and grow up to five feet long. They can dive to a depth of three hundred feet to hunt for food.

GREENLAND SHARK

Greenland sharks grow to twenty-three feet in length, and it is believed they have the longest life span of any vertebrate, nearly four hundred years. They can be seen in Arctic waters at the surface and as deep as four thousand feet. They are slow-moving ocean scavengers, but also ambush seals asleep at the surface.

WALRUS

Walruses can live for forty years and grow to be twelve feet long. They can dive to 260 feet below the surface, where they use their whiskers to search for clams as well as worms, snails, crabs, and small octopuses hiding in the seabed.

NARWHAL

Narwhals are one of the deepest-diving whales, and at times may hunt fish and squid a mile or more below the surface. They grow to twelve to eighteen feet in length, not including the males' long tusks, and may live for ninety years.

BOWHEAD WHALE

Bowhead whales may live for two hundred years or more and grow as long as sixty feet. They can dive to five hundred feet deep, and they feed on a rich mix of small animals, called zooplankton, that they filter from the water.